merry Ch

W9-BSF-103

The Book
Of A Thousand
Thimbles

By

MYRTLE LUNDQUIST

Published by
Wallace-Homestead Book Co.
P. O. Box BI
Des Moines, Iowa 50304

Copyright 1970
Myrtle Lundquist

Photography By
Duree Studio
Ottumwa, Iowa

ISBN: 0-87069-008-6

Fourth Printing

Printed By
WALLACE-HOMESTEAD CO.
Des Moines, Iowa
U.S.A.

ACKNOWLEDGMENTS

The advice, encouragement and expert assistance of the following are especially and gratefully acknowledged:

Mrs. Bertha S. Baker
Mrs. Jeannette Brownell
Mrs. Alva Byron
Mrs. Grace Cottrell
Mrs. Thomas J. Cullen
Mrs. Ida Dornbos
Mrs. Thomas J. Gallagher
Miss Elisa Galban
Mrs. E. A. Heath
Mrs. Myrtle Holstead
Mr. Ellis L. Isom
Miss Portia Mary Lee
Mrs. Anna E. Johnson
Mr. George Kull
Mrs. Paul Lorenz
Mrs. Charles Lundquist

Mrs. L. N. Marr
Mrs. Marie Pendergast Mints
Mr. Thomas M. Mints
Mrs. Rollin MacDonald
Mrs. Edward McNamara
Mrs. Josephine Miller
Miss Jane Nystrom
Miss Willa Nanzig
Mrs. Thornton L. Page
Mrs. Ben J. Parsons
Mrs. Nancy Peters
Mrs. Lina Schreiber
Mrs. Edgar Sampson
Mrs. Donald H. Scott
Mrs. Bernie Tyson
Mrs. William B. Weiss
Mrs. Madeline Webber

T. J. Cullen, Jeweler
W. Eppel, Simons Bros. & Co.
J. H. Gebelein, Gebelein Silversmiths
Helen Taylor, Cellini Shop
Mrs. Robert P. Schwartz
Mrs. E. P. Sickels
Mrs. Dorothy Bell Booty, Booty Photos

Boston Museum of Fine Arts, Boston, Mass.
British Museum, London
Field Museum of Natural History, Chicago
Huntington Historical Society, Huntington, L. I.
Metropolitan Museum of Art, New York
Victoria and Albert Museum, London
Yale University Art Gallery, New Haven, Conn.

A special thank you also to all who have added treasured thimbles to the select company comprising the collection featured in this book.

CONTENTS

Acknowledgments

Preface

Chapter One   On Collecting 7

Chapter Two   Thimbles Defined 9

Chapter Three   Thimbles in Museums.. 11

Chapter Four   Metalsmiths 13

Chapter Five   Periods of Style... 17

Chapter Six   Engraving 21

Chapter Seven   Thimble Makers 23

Chapter Eight   Marks 25

Chapter Nine   Categories 33

Chapter Ten   "Just a Thimble Full"... 35

Chapter Eleven   Hints to Beginning Collectors............................... 37

4

PREFACE

BEGINNINGS

"How did you happen to start?" is a question frequently asked of a collector. A single piece of china or glass that belonged to one's ancestors, a childhood gift from an aunt and uncle, or a fascinating piece seen on a what-not have impelled many a collector on a lifetime quest. As with the proverbial Chinese journey beginning with a single step, comprehensive collections may start with one particular piece.

It was a chance remark that set a search for a thousand different thimbles in motion. Years ago, when there was a custom among advertisers to present a small premium for a box top and a dime, a gadget manufacturer asked for a design that would appeal to women. This was to be made of plastic for a very small cost. There was the stipulation that only patentable objects would be acceptable.

Long fingernails were in vogue at the time, and there was submitted among other innovations the design of a thimble with a pocket extending from the top into which a long fingernail would fit. The manufacturer liked the design and planned to use it, remarking, "My grandmother had a thimble with her name on it but it was like every other thimble I've ever seen. There hasn't been a new design in 2000 years."

Later, the patent was refused because someone had patented a thimble of somewhat different design which served the same purpose. It had an open slot at the top for the nail to slip through. This thimble was never produced as far as is known.

So suddenly all that was left of the incident was a consciousness of thimbles which has never diminished.

Thereafter, every thimble within reach was examined. It became apparent that for so simple an object, there were many varieties. Old button boxes, machine drawers, and sewing cases were raided. It was thought after a while that one might find a thousand different thimbles. The search began.

Friends presented thimbles that had belonged to relatives—old ones, new ones, fancy ones, plain ones, worn ones, foreign ones—and they were cataloged.

"This thimble belonged to my grandmother who lived through the Chicago fire." "This one came from Sweden in 1830." "This one was my mother's confirmation present at fifteen. She started her hope chest with it." "This was an engagement troth as was the custom in some foreign countries".

So the collection grew. Thimbles accumulated at first in boxes, drawers and jars. It became difficult to find a certain one immediately.

It seems appropriate to mention here that collections worth having warrant attractive storage space adequate to the size and preservation of the object. Many beautiful collections rest in boxes on shelves or in attics. Collections should be accessible for enjoyment and to share with others.

There then came to light a fine old thread cabinet formerly used in a general store for spools of thread. This particular one, coincidentally, is comprised of seven drawers, each containing 156 grooves for a total of 1092 spaces, long since filled with thimbles.

Another container is an old dental cabinet of cherry wood with 27 shallow drawers which conveniently houses thimbles and thimble cases. These pieces of furniture are not easy to obtain, but anyone who can find thimbles should be able to provide a suitable receptacle.

In fact, with a collector who really has become enamored of thimbles, containers will continue to overflow to other cases, curio cabinets, drawers, and jars all over again.

"Case of a thousand thimbles"

One drawer of case

Chapter One

ON COLLECTING

Those with an interest in tracing clues to the customs of other times, places and situations will find collecting most rewarding. There is satisfaction in searching and finding. Much of the pleasure derives from the quest.

Children enjoy gathering stones and seashells. Most people retain some mementos related to happy experiences.

Associations with the past survive in the tangible items one collects. From similarities and differences, relationships are found which reach far into history.

A real collector keeps searching for still more varieties of his objective, and with thimbles the quest may be well rewarded. A thimble is a romantic object and with reflection takes on character. It has become a popular collectors' item.

Antique dealers seek to learn the trends in collecting. It seems that anything may become a collectors' item if it is interesting enough and if there are large numbers available from which to select. Among collectibles popular today are:

animals	cups and saucers	magazines	salt shakers
art	furniture	majolica	sewing needs
books	glassware	pencils	silver
bottles	jewelry	pitchers	souvenirs
buttons	hatpins	postcards	spoons
campaign data	insulators	pottery	stamps
china	license plates	prints	thimbles
coins	linen	rocks	woodenware

Interest in thimbles along with other collectors' items has increased in the last several years. Thimble collectors' groups are growing in number. Some of these associations exchange data by correspondence.

It is the purpose of this book to classify thimbles for the convenience of collectors and for the entertainment of laymen.

An attempt is made to represent general groups of thimbles and to describe individually some significant characteristics.

From the pyramids to the Parthenon, from stone to sterling silver, thimbles have played a part in our heritage. They are interesting to examine and research, their size makes them easy to accumulate, and they are available in many varieties. As with any collectors' item, rare or ornate pieces are expensive. However, large numbers may be collected at nominal prices, and in the case of those bearing advertisements, for no cost at all. Advertising plastics and metals indicate current trends in our culture.

The point of view is taken here that items from many times, places and economic situations are more representative of social history than an assemblage limited to those of elegant artistry and fine quality. Included here are examples of thimbles from those crudely made of whatever material was available, to the luxurious product of the finest craftsmen.

While penetrating the many facets of collecting from a personal viewpoint, one compares the pinpoint of the present with our heritage and perhaps reflects upon our obligations to the future. Creativity in any form is born of courage and adventure.

Since thimble collecting is a comparatively new avocation, there must be many items of historical interest still undiscovered or unrecognized.

Chapter Two

THIMBLES DEFINED

There is something inspiring about thimbles. The association with sewing leads one into the world of the ornamental and singular as well as the utilitarian.

The sociological aspects of thimble collecting are fascinating, and many thimbles tell a story. They lead in retrospect to the people who owned these treasures and were perhaps more interesting than the objects themselves.

By definition, a thimble is a sewing tool, a small bell-shaped implement devised to protect the finger on which it is worn, as well as to save motion. It has been estimated that about 50 percent of effort is saved by using a thimble. Without one, two operations are required, one to push the needle partway and another to pull the needle through the fabric.

Thimbles are usually designed to fit over the end of the finger, or as a cylinder with no top, called a tailor's thimble, sometimes worn on the thumb. With open top thimbles, the tip of the finger is free to feel the needle and material. The word "thimble" is believed by some to derive from "thumb-bell".

A thimble may be called one of the first signs of civilization. Necessity was an urge even in cave dweller days. A thimble has been needed by those who sew a great deal since the first designers joined leaves together. Cavewomen "started where they were with what they had" which may have been a piece of bone from an animal's leg, a stone, or a twig. They needed protection from a piercing bone needle when they combined skins. At any rate, one must concede that thimbles of one sort or another have probably played an interesting part in the progress of civilization.

The urge to better one's self by way of comfort and adornment appears early in human history. Nature inspired the first designs as human beings adapted to environment and began to seek ways to make work easier. So it is that one contrives what one needs. Cavewomen started with a thimble. This was a beginning.

Thimbles have been made of almost any kind of metal or material one can mention. Since many were custom made, the imagination took long flights to create individuality unlimited.

Thimbles have been made of:

aluminum	gold	leather	porcelain
bone	horn	nickel	rubber
brass	iron	onyx	silver
china	ivory	pewter	steel
enamel	jade	pinchbeck	tortoiseshell
glass	lead	plastic	wood

Several metals were sometimes combined.

Early bronze Greek and Roman thimbles were found at Pompeii and Herculaneum after their rediscovery in 1738 and subsequent excavation. These cities were buried by a volcanic eruption in 79 A.D. Some of these thimbles were made of bronze cast in moulds and others were made from sheets of metal.

Sailors have used thimbles for centuries. The great sails of early galleons required constant sewing and mending. A sailor's leather thimble protects the palm of the hand and is laced across the back. These are used today by sailing enthusiasts and may be purchased in sporting goods stores.

An elderly Norwegian sailor in northern Wisconsin treasures the thimble he used for years "rounding the Horn". He has never seen the eastern seaboard of North America. Wisconsin has the climate of his native country so he settled there in retirement. (Note to collectors: The thimble is not for sale.)

Most thimbles are made in two parts, the side and top being soldered together. Early indentations were handmade and spacing is irregular. Later indentations were made with a gnarled roller. For decoration, bands were added separately or rolled on the base metal. Several metals are used in some thimbles for lining and durability. It is known that some early craftsmen made thimbles from a single flat piece of metal, shaping it against a "stamp". Others "turned" their work for more ornamental effects.

Ivory thimbles were made in two or sometimes three parts. Onyx thimbles were carved from a single piece.

Let the galleries and museums preserve the rarest thimbles for posterity. Here all varieties are welcome with their folklore and intrinsic evidence of bygone days. Early immigrants brought thimbles to America, and these small mementos of their homeland must have been dearly treasured.

Grandmother's thimble may have been of gold, well worn from sewing buttons on little boys' shirts or ruffles on little girls' frocks. In her day there were hope chests to fill, wedding dresses to sew, quilts to stitch, baby clothes to prepare, all touched by the thimble. An older thimble takes one back to the part it may have played in events of its time. With modern thimbles one associates present needs and aesthetic values.

The collection of thimbles described in this book is democratic in that it tends to represent a cross-section of people, the way they pursued happiness, and their contributions to society in general.

Chapter Three

THIMBLES IN MUSEUMS

Records regarding old thimbles exist in documents, letters, museums, libraries, old newspapers, and magazines.

The *Boston Museum of Fine Arts* owns a gold thimble made by Paul Revere in 1805 for a daughter. Her name, Maria Revere Balestier, is beautifully engraved in a short stroke style fashionable at the time. Documents indicate that Mr. Revere made two thimbles for two daughters. The whereabouts of the second one is unknown, if indeed it still exists. The following letter written to John Revere by the brother of Maria's husband is preserved at the museum. The word "sister-in-law" was not commonly used in 1879.

Brattleboro, Dec. 23, 1879

My dear John

Among my brother's effects which I found in a Washington bank was a gold thimble being, as I was informed, one of two which Paul Revere made with his own hands for his daughters.

Thinking you would value this thimble both as a memorial of your famous grand-father and of my beloved sister, Maria, I beg your acceptance of it.

I remain always

Affectionately yours
J. W. Balestier

P.S. The thimble will go by Express.
To John Revere, Esq.
    Boston

Yale University Art Gallery in New Haven, Connecticut, holds a gold thimble made by Jacob Hurd, an early American metalsmith, 1702-1758. The thimble was presented to the Gallery with The Garvan Collection made up of 17th, 18th, and 19th Century American silver, gold, furniture, glass, and painting.

At the *Field Museum of Chicago,* a Klamath Indian woman's dress of yellow buckskin, heavily beaded at the yoke, is adorned with 41 old brass thimbles as pendants from the blue beaded fringe. The dress was said to be about 100 years old when acquired by the museum in November 1900. The Klamath Reservation is in Oregon. The thimbles are all brass but of different sizes and not identical. None are worn. It may be surmised that an itinerant peddler reached the Intermountain Indian tribes with his wagon of wares and Indian women traded with him. If the dress was 100 years old in 1900, the thimbles were made by a metalsmith of our early history. The costume is exhibited in a glass case and at this time it is impossible to find marks of identification. Perhaps some time a thimble collector wll have access to the thimbles with a jeweler's loop, and the work of some early thimble maker will be identified.

The *Metropolitan Museum* in New York exhibits a stone thimble from the South Pyramid which may be the oldest identifiable thimble extant. Also on exhibit are a German thimble dated 1577 and a 19th Century French thimble, both indicating designs of their time.

Bronze thimbles from Pompeii are among treasures at the *British Museum* in London.

The following quotation is from the catalogue of the *British Museum* in London:

"Thimbles are mentioned as early as the twelfth century, and had been used from more ancient times. They were doubtless made of bone as well as of metal, and leather was also employed. Latten thimbles are referred to in the thirteenth century, but actual objects are difficult to date owing to the general similarity of known examples; apparently the more ancient specimens were less finely pitted on the outer surface than those of later date. In Queen Elizabeth's inventory appear:

'a nedell case of cristall garnysshed with
silver gilt, with two thumbles in it';

silver thimbles of an early date are rare, but they were apparently common in the seventeenth century; a silver thimble of the time of Charles II is in Table Case, Bay XV."

The *Victoria and Albert Museum* in London exhibits several 12th to 13th Century Hispano-Moresque bronze thimbles, reminiscent of Moorish mosques. The indentations on one of these are unusually large.

Also exhibited are a beautiful Chelsea porcelain thimble and one of English enamel. An 18th Century Italian thimble is a fine example of wirework ornamentation.

Gold thimble made by Paul Revere in 1805 for his daughter, inscribed "Maria Revere Balestier". Engraving is done in short strokes and the top is hand punched. Courtesy, Museum of Fine Arts, Boston. Gift of Mrs. Henry B. Chapin and Ward H. R. Revere.

Gold thimble made by Jacob Hurd (American 1702-1758). Courtesy of Yale University Art Gallery, Mabel Brady Garvan Collection.

Egyptian thimble, Stone. Dynasty XX-XXII. Lisht; South Pyramid. Courtesy Metropolitan Museum of Art. Museum Excavations 1911; Rogers Fund, 1911.

Case of Intermountain Tribes Indian costumes. Woman's dress at far left is of yellow buckskin heavily beaded at the top. Forty-one brass thimbles hang as pendants from blue beaded fringe decorating the yoke. The dress was acquired by the museum in November 1900 from the Klamath Reservation, Oregon, USA. The costume was believed to be 100 years old when acquired. Courtesy The Field Museum of Natural History, Chicago.

French thimble, 19th century. Courtesy The Metropolitan Museum of Art. Bequest of Mrs. Maria P. James, 1911.

German thimble dated 1577. Augsburg. Courtesy The Metropolitan Museum of Art. Rogers Fund 1910.

English thimbles from as early as the time of Charles II (1660). Actual dating is difficult because of similarity of known examples. Apparently the oldest ones were less finely pitted. Used through the courtesy of the Antiquities Department, British Museum, London.

Chapter Four

METALSMITHS

Goldsmiths and silversmiths have worked with metals for thousands of years. "Silversmith" has come to mean a person who works with gold and silver. "Metalsmith" refers to persons who work with any metal.

European homelands influenced early silversmiths in America. In New York, silversmiths followed Dutch designs. Silversmiths in the English colonies followed traditional patterns. So it was with the French, Germans, Scandinavians, and other settlers.

The American melting pot inevitably combined details in basic forms and several patterns can be noted in single pieces of colonial silver.

There were more than 400 silversmiths working in the American colonies. Some phases of their ancient craft are interesting to ponder.

Gold was mentioned by Moses 1,500 years before Christ. Candlesticks, lamps, instruments of gold, and an altar of incense of refined gold are mentioned. There were gods made of gold, also chains, rings, cherubims, and gold beaten into thin sheets.

Gold is found among the oldest Egyptian monuments. The Chinese have known gold from the beginning of their history. It is found all over the world but not in large deposits.

At the same time in what is now South America, the Incas were accumulating large quantities of gold. There are records of five-foot statues cast of solid gold.

Malleability, ductility, tenacity, color, and hardness are useful properties of gold and other precious metals.

Gold is the most malleable of all metals and silver is next. Gold can be beaten into leaves 200,000th of an inch in thickness. Ductility is that property of a metal which yields to a force that tends to draw it into wire. Silver for gold-lace, when gilded, can be drawn into wire 500th of an inch thick.

Gold of 24 karats, or pure gold, is too soft to work well and wear well, so it must be alloyed with other metal. What is known as 18-karat gold, three-quarters gold and one-quarter alloy, fulfills the requirements best. Gold standards of lesser gold content are 15, 12 and 9 karats.

The word "sterling" derives from money coined in the East of Germany which, on account of its purity, was called Easterling money in England as all inhabitants of that part of Germany were called Easterlings. Some of these people carried their skills to London to improve coinage. Thus, the name "sterling" designates good money or anything genuine. The term sterling, or standard, has the same meaning when referring to gold or silver.

The word "standard" denotes in the case of gold an alloy of 22/24 parts pure gold to 2/24 parts of another metal. In silver, it means 222/240 parts of pure silver to 18/240 parts of copper. The object of the hallmark is to give a guarantee to the public that all plate thus marked is equal to money, weight for weight.

Copper and Brass

Copper is a mined malleable metal which can be spread or rolled into sheets. Brass is manufactured of copper and zinc.

Coppersmiths and braziers worked in all metals, brazier having referred originally to a smith working in sheet brass. Founders were skilled artisans in early America.

Craftsmen in seaports manufactured items for ships. Paul Revere made the sheet copper for The Constitution. Coppersmiths living inland produced utensils for home use. Names on copper thimbles are sometimes imprinted by intaglio dies. Copper and brass thimbles are used for advertising.

The secrets of the copper trade were kept for centuries by agreement between master and apprentice until "The Art of Coppersmithing" by John Fuller was published in 1893.

Aluminum

Aluminum is a white metal used extensively in making advertising thimbles. From sewing machines to bakery goods, the attention of the lady of the house is solicited. Colored bands are yellow, blue, orange, green, and red in varying styles. Numerous types of borders are used. Decorations are similar to silver and brass patterns. Some ladies prefer these aluminum thimbles because of the light weight. Advertisements appear in raised letters which remain legible after paint has worn off. An aluminum thimble marked "Austria" indicates that this medium was used prior to World War I.

Processes

Various processes are used for decorating metals. One might establish some placement of a thimble in time by the type of ornament used.

Chasing is done with punches. In this method none of the metal is removed. Flat-chasing refers to shallow marks.

Cut-card: A thin mask of silver applied to other metal.

Damascene is a form of ornament with inlayed designs of another metal.

Embossing is the hammering from the outside against forms inside the metal to raise the design in relief. (Repoussé and embossing are the same process.)

Enameling is the use of colored substances as coatings in decoration. The name derives from smelting. French artisans were masters of enameling.

Engraving involves the removal of a part of the metal with graving tools. This type of ornament is adaptable to lettering and design.

Filigree is executed with fine metal wire, usually leaving open spaces.

Filleting is the application of bands.

Gadrooning is an edge of convex lines, or gadroons, made over a mould shaped for the purpose.

Moulding is casting in a mould and this is efficient for some pieces of decoration such as cherubs, pineapples, or raised flowers.

Niello refers to a very old process of filling lined patterns on gold or silver with a black metal. Silver, copper, and lead are melted together and sulphur added which blackens the composition.

Stamping by dies is used for repeating a decoration on bands which are then soldered to a piece.

Chapter Five
PERIODS OF STYLE

Periods of design in metal smithing seem to correlate with economic and cultural advances.

Monks worked at goldsmithing in monasteries for centuries and much of the production was of a religious nature. Much old ecclesiastical silver made in the abbeys was melted down to pay for wars. Some existing magnificent pieces evidence the excellence of the artistry.

Goldsmiths organized the first guilds in the 12th Century. Lords of the manor demanded silver and gold objects as symbols of power. Platters and cups of gold and silver were signs of wealth.

In the 15th century, Renaissance styles were influenced by silversmiths of Italy, France, and Germany.

As Queen Elizabeth reigned in prosperity, designs changed to a lavish splendor much in demand at the time.

The High Standard Period, about 1697-1720, derives from the higher standard of silver required by an Act of Parliament in 1696 fixing prices for articles bearing the London hallmark. The standard of metal for silver articles was raised above the standard for coinage, thus making it unprofitable to melt coins to make articles. During the High Standard Period, therefore, silver was necessarily softer. Change to a more simple decoration ensued. Flutings, spirals, and foliage were popular. The decoration was done mostly by cut-card work.

It should be noted that a lesser content of silver with alloy is not used necessarily to reduce costliness. Alloys are added to harden metal and to increase durability.

Silver of the Rococo Period, 1720-1770, is lavishly ornate, usually all-over in design, using shells and marine objects. With the return of the standard silver, rococo work developed to extravagant use of scrolls, sprays of flowers, and ribbons. Rococo stemmed from the Oriental. Thimbles of this period are heavy with ornament.

The Classic Period, about 1770 to 1825, was influenced by the excavation of Pompeii and Herculaneum in Italy. The classic Greek and Roman forms in architecture and jewelry were much admired and soon became popular. Silver of this period bears the Greek fret meander, rosettes, swags of drapery, acanthus leaves, honeysuckle, bead borders, festoons of fruit, foliage, and medallions.

During the Revolutionary War period and afterward, it seems that American silversmiths developed a typically independent style, less lavish than the Empire Period designs of France. The rococo and classic patterns were modified and became simple but rich in line and artistry.

Design and Decoration

The variety of decoration on thimbles is a source of challenge to the collector.

Borders range from a plain edge to elaborate cherubic bands and geometric strapwork. All-over designs are of wide variety.

Basic designs and patterns drawn from nature are used repeatedly on borders of thimbles. The more ornate bands are applied to the base metal. When manufacturers began to use mechanical processes, borders were rolled on, reserving a space or shield for a name or initials.

Motifs

Thimbles may be allocated by symbolic patterns which in turn can be subdivided:

Acanthus: Old Greek. Leaves from the acanthus plant.

Anthemion: Greek. Honeysuckle.

Classic: Designs taken from Greek and Roman objects excavated at Pompeii and Herculaneum.

Cornucopia: Empire Period. Horn of plenty, fruits and flowers.

Crests: Heraldic decoration. Some shields for monograms on thimbles take the form of family crests.

Faceted: Small, smooth surfaces similar to the facets on a gem.

Floral: Conventional examples are similar to the following:

Blossoms	Daisy	Roses
Chrysanthemums	Forget-me-not	Shamrocks
Clover	Fuchsia	Thumbelina
Cosmos	Lily of the valley	Wild rose
Dahlia	Pansies	Zinnia

Thumbelina of the zinnia family is found on many old thimbles.

Good luck symbols: Horseshoes, wishbones, clovers.

Palm leaves: Greek.

Pelleting or pickling: All-over dotted background similar to shot marks.

Rococo: Very heavy and ornate.

Romantic: Birds, bowknots, doves, hearts, moons, stars, forget-me-nots.

Scrolls: Greek.

Shell: Greek.

Stone tops: Amethyst, carnelian, moonstone, and other semi-precious stones were used extensively as tops for thimbles in the 18th and 19th centuries. Modern thimbles sometimes use synthetic stones.

Strapwork was used by Dutch smiths in New York and is not found on pieces made elsewhere. Interlacing strapwork was used with foliage, birds, fruits, and other objects.

Waffle weave: Squared pattern of indentations.

Wirework: Silver wire applied in design or outline, sometimes filled with enamel. Fine wire is also woven into designs for filigree.

Chapter Six

ENGRAVING

Engraving is an ancient art. The signet ring or seal dates back thousands of years. There are references to Jacob leaving his signet with his bracelet and staff.

Joseph Struitt, 1749-1802, writes in "An Essay on the Art of Engraving . . ." that seal rings were used thousands of years ago and that the engraver of signets was mentioned by Moses. These were intaglio insignia, the forerunner of modern seals. Mr. Struitt wondered why it took until around 1450 A.D. before a man in Germany named Gutenberg began to use seals as movable type in a printing process.

As a means of dating, engraving on thimbles is not infallible because artists used different styles of lettering in a given period. In cases of custom made thimbles, it is probable that the style of letters was selected to conform to the decoration. If the name were long, smaller letters were used. Initials or monograms were used to indicate personal ownership and on thimbles the space was extremely limited.

Many styles of letters and forms of lines may be found in 17th and 18th century examples. The engraver of early woodcuts was a skilled craftsman. A monogram on a thimble was a simple task for him.

Popular types of engraving include hair-lines, shaded lines, beauty-cut, dog tooth, slanted script, vertical script, ribbon letters, Roman letters, and the wide-cut for fill-in work using cross-lines, cross-wriggles, or pickling.

Fancy ribbon cut monograms appear on antique gold thimbles. Short hair-line strokes were used frequently but wearing of the metal lessens legibility.

The engraver's art as applied to decoration of metals is only one phase of engraving.

It is the names and dates inscribed on some old thimbles that renders them extremely interesting. Contrary to hallmarks, there is no definite criterion for determining dates from engravings, but the subject may be pursued by matching styles and patterns.

One can, however, assume that the given names themselves were popular during certain times. The spelling also may be an indication of the period. The following notes are indicative of possible interpretations:

"Zylphia" bears no date but this spelling can be related to "Sylvia". It should be recalled that a century ago many people were illiterate and phonetic spelling was the order of the time.

One thimble bears the inscription "Zana 1894". The name is unusual but has been found elsewhere.

The name "Daisey", which dropped the "e" long since, was popular in the 1890s.

Chapter Seven

THIMBLE MAKERS

Among early silversmiths whose names are linked with thimble making by documentary evidence or by thimbles which still exist are:

Nicholas van Benschoten of Amsterdam during the 17th century.

John Lofting, Islington near London, a Dutchman in 1695, started the first metal thimble manufacturing business, from which he acquired a fortune. His watermill workshop was mentioned by Daniel Defoe.

Lady smiths who achieved fame in Great Britain during the George III era, 1760-1820, were Hester and Anne Bateman, members of the well-known silversmith family which included Jonathan, Peter, and William. All fulfilled apprenticeships and were listed by famous silversmiths of their time.

No records of early American lady smiths have been found. It seems that women of silversmithing families in the colonies confined their activities to care and nurture of apprentices bound to their menfolk.

In America, the following names are found in advertisements and documents relating to early metalsmithing. Only those linked in some way with thimbles are included:

Benjamin Halsted, silversmith of New York, advertised thimbles of gold, silver, and pinchbeck with steel tops, in 1766.

Charles Shipman of New York advertised ivory thimbles in 1767.

Paul Revere of Boston made thimbles along with other fine pieces of gold and silver. He worked in copper also, having made the sheets used on The Constitution. Mr. Revere was a man of many talents, a superb metalsmith. He worked with many metals. His "Sons of Liberty" bowl is one of the most treasured pieces of historic silver in America. This is owned by the Boston Museum of Fine Arts.

James Peters of Philadelphia advertised thimbles in 1824.

George, David, and Nathan Platt of Huntington, L. I., manufactured thimbles in the 1820s. The Huntington Historical Society has a thimble inscribed "S. Platt" made by David Platt for his wife. David Platt and Nathaniel Potter manufactured thimbles from 1828 to 1835.

Gorham, Webster and Price had a thimble manufactory in Rhode Island in the 1830s.

Ezra Prime, who served his apprenticeship to George Platt, established a thimble factory in 1837 and made thimbles until 1890. Many thousands of Prime thimbles were distributed over this period. Three Prime brothers were associated with thimbles and supplied dealers in this country and abroad. Prime thimbles were well known in the middle and late 1800s. No touchmark identifies them.

John Roshore became associated with the Primes when the Prime brothers' partnership ended. He later became affiliated with Brewster Wood, Jr., a cousin of the Platts and the Primes. Many inter-family relationships resulted from young men marrying into the mastersmith's family or because smiths took sons or nephews as apprentices. Proximity of the families and a common interest encouraged romance. Interwoven names of descendants and heirs read like a novel.

Edward Woodhull Ketcham, a cousin of the Primes, manufactured thimbles from 1875 in partnership with Hugh McDougall. The Ketcham-McDougall trademark appears in the apex of their thimbles, a large K with M to the left and D to the right with a small C on the upper limb of K. Ketcham and McDougall were among leading manufacturers of thimbles until 1932 when the item was discontinued.

These early American silversmiths were not bound by any law to mark their goods as was required in England. Much colonial silver is not marked, but collections in museums reveal fine workmanship.

Simons Brothers of Philadelphia, silversmiths since 1839, are the only manufacturers of gold and silver thimbles in the United States today. Their trademark is a large English "S" in a shield, found in the apex of their thimbles.

The legislative act requiring that imports bear the name of the country of origin was passed in 1897, which provides one means of dating thimbles. This requirement also appears in the Tariff Act of 1930. Therefore, thimbles bearing the name of a country probably were imported after 1897. However, some small items, including thimbles, were exempt from this requirement.

Among foreign thimbles there were many with no markings. It should be noted that thimbles purchased in foreign countries and brought here as gifts often bear no identification. Many of the simple utilitarian variety are similar to those used all over the world.

During the Industrial Revolution, which began about 1760 in England and later in other countries, various machines replaced hand tools and products were made in large quantities.

As with many collectors' items and antiques, identifying thimbles becomes a challenge which sends one down many roads of reference. Books on silversmiths, metals, marks, engraving, and design are available and useful. They frequently overlap and one finds another tangent to travel in his exploration.

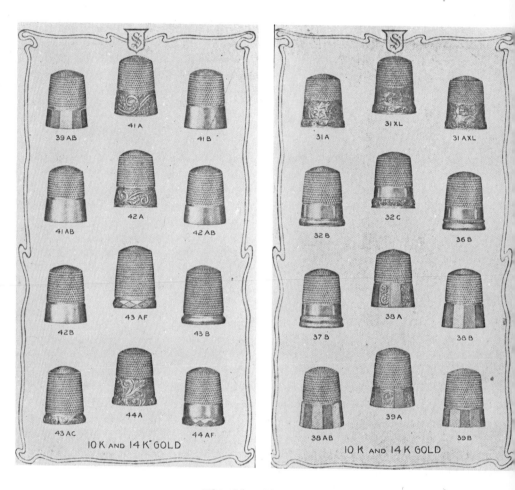

Thimbles Since 1839

Simons Bros. Company, Thimble Makers, established in 1839 by George Simons, a Welsh immigrant, is the only concern in America still making sterling and gold thimbles. The craft has been handed down from father to son and through apprenticeships at the old thimble factory in Philadelphia and gold and silver thimbles are made the same way as they were when the shop opened although today electricity empowers the simple machines to knurl over a thousand thimble sides a day. This is only one of a dozen processes required to finish gold or silver thimbles. Some methods are carefully guarded by the craftsmen. In early contracts the Simons Bros. Company promised to "teach the art, trade, and mystery" of the craft. A number of World War II veterans have served apprenticeships at Simons Bros. Company.

At one time there were six manufacturers of thimbles and each used his own set of sizes. All had sizes slightly different ranging from 1 to 18, the most used being 8-9-10-11.

At the turn of the century, custom made diamond studded gold thimbles sold for $150.00.

The reproductions are from an old Simons Bros. Company catalogue. Their trademark, the English "S" in a shield, appears at the top of the pages. There have been variations over the years but the English "S' is easily identifiable in the apex of thousands of thimbles.

26

Chapter Eight
MARKS

Historical societies engage in preserving objects of former generations and any collection may add to the dissemination of knowledge. A collector becomes discriminating as he studies marks of many varieties.

Librarians, historians, jewelers, silversmiths, reference books, magazines, books, letters, pictures, old engravings are all possible means of identifying an object.

Identifications can be made by maker's marks, hallmarks, touchmarks, trademarks, the word "sterling," silver and gold marks, the figure 800 or other numerals in the 800s.

Maker's Marks

Perhaps pride in craftsmanship prompted ancient makers to mark their work. It may be that competitors began to produce an inferior product and the maker's mark was a sign of reputed quality. The mark could be any kind of insignia or letter. Maker's marks exist on treasures excavated from tombs dating to ancient civilizations.

Goldsmith and Silversmith Marks

Gold and silversmiths of various countries have been regulated by laws since the 12th century and the guilds of the middle ages were organized to maintain certain standards.

Hallmarks

"Hallmark" refers to stamps indicating a standard used in marking gold and silver articles assayed by the Goldsmiths' Company of London. The word derives from Goldsmiths' "Hall" plus "mark". Four marks evidence the maker's name, place of origin, sterling mark, and date.

To identify hallmarks on thimbles, it is essential to search reference books on marks. London, Birmingham, Norwich, and other English guilds can be identified through tables of marks. Irish and Scottish marks, as well as continental marks, are tabled in books on marks. One soon becomes familiar with standard marks, the lion passant, Britannia, and lion rampant. Date marks establish the year the piece was stamped by an assay office.

Sterling

"Sterling" represents the standard for gold and silver coin usually .925 silver and .075 alloy. The word "sterling" on American silver was used after the 1860s.

"800"

The numeral "800" or any figure in the 800's places a piece in a category commonly called "Continental Silver". Several European countries use these figures. Because thimbles are exempt from the law requiring that the country of origin be imprinted thereon, the foreign source is not identifiable. The figures simply indicate a lesser quantity of silver with alloy. 880 represents .880 of silver and .120 alloy. Thousands of thimbles bear these figures. None of them are American made. This does not mean that thimbles with the 800 numeral are less desirable. Some foreign makers seem to feel that the lesser quantity of silver makes the article more durable.

Formerly, Scandinavian countries and Germany used 830/100 Fine as a standard. However, 830 does not necessarily indicate these countries as the place of origin. This simply indicates the silver content.

The word "coin" was used on an article to indicate solid coin silver, 892.4 Fine, according to United States Mint standard.

Touchmarks

During colonial days, it was the custom for the purchaser to take silver coin to the metalsmiths for made-to-order products. The integrity of the smith was highly regarded. Thimbles made at that time were not marked by the maker unless he chose to add his touchmark.

"Touchmark" refers to a stamp put on metal after testing for purity. The word also refers to the die for impressing the mark. Few such dies used by early metalsmiths exist because it was the custom to destroy them to prevent further use. Touchmarks are a means for identifying some early American gold and silver pieces. These marks were not required by any law in the colonies but many metalsmiths used their initials alone or the first initial and surname in a border or shield.

Touchmarks usually appear on the border.

Some smiths used a mark similar to hallmarks but there is no significance of date as there was no registration of marks. Such a list would be invaluable to researchers today.

Trademarks

"Trademark" represents a name, symbol, or mark used by a manufacturer or merchant to identify his products. A trademark does not necessarily refer to the maker. These are usually registered, the first in this country having been entered in 1871. Again, a certain fine quality of manufacture is assigned to the product by a well-reputed trademark.

Many silversmiths had brought their talents from European countries. There were no trade schools. Young men served long apprenticeships, often from 14 to 21 years of age, to master silversmiths. After serving their time, they frequently went into business for themselves or into partnership with another smith.

Trademarks Which Might Be Found In Thimbles

 R. Blackinton & Company
North Attelboro, Mass.

 D. C. Bourquin
Port Richmond, N. Y.

 Thomas S. Brogan
New York, N. Y.

 Joseph F. Chatellier
Newark, N. J.

 S. Cottle Co.
New York, N. Y.

 Crane & Thevrer

C.M.C.

Crown Manufacturing Co.
North Attelboro, Mass.

Crown Silver Co. Inc.
New York, N. Y.

E. S. C. O.

Eagle Silver Co.
Providence, R. I.

George C. Gebelein
Boston, Mass.

STERLING G

F. S. Gilbert
North Attelboro, Mass.

Goldstein & Swank Co.
Worcester, Mass.

Goldsmith Stern
or
Stern Bros. Co.
New York, N. Y.

Gorham Corporation
Providence, R. I.

 A. T. Gunner Mfg. Co.
Attelboro, Mass.

 William W. Hayden Co.
Newark, N. J.

 George A. Henckel & Co.
New York, N. Y.

 Frederick S. Hoffman
Brooklyn, N. Y.

 C. F. Kees & Co.
Newark, N. J.

Ketcham & McDougall
Brooklyn, N. Y.

 C. Klank & Sons
Baltimore, Md.

 The Frank Kursh & Son Co.
Newark, N. J.

 Frank T. May Co.
New York, N. Y.
Rutherford, N. J.

 Reed & Barton
Taunton, Mass.

 Wm. Rogers Mfg. Co.
Hartford, Conn.

Simons Bros.
Philadelphia, Pa.

 Isaac Swope & Co.

 Towle Silversmiths
Newburyport, Mass.

 Chas. L. Trout & Co.

 Wayne Silver Co.
Honesdale, Pa.

 Webster Company
North Attelboro, Mass.

 Wortz & Voorhis
New York, N. Y.

Chapter Nine

CATEGORIES

An organization of categories is a matter of choice. Selection may be difficult as some thimbles are eligible for several places. Some of the groups included here may stimulate interest among kindred collectors.

Animals: Horses, camels, buffaloes, dinosaurs. (Sinclair Oil Company advertised with plastic thimbles using the dinosaur trademark.)

Buildings: Castles, cathedrals, farmhouses.

Borders: Floral, geometric, sentimental and romantic designs.

Brass: Many brass thimbles are imports, usually of the longer type extending below the first joint of the finger. Some beautiful decorative brass thimbles originated in Austria and Germany.

Campaign: Aluminum, nickel, brass, and plastic thimbles are used for campaign publicity. One collector's item is a plastic thimble inscribed "Nixon for Senator".

Children's: Small thimbles from sewing boxes. Thimbles with nursery rhymes.

Cities and States: Advertising thimbles sometimes bear the city and state of origin.

Commemorative: A thimble commemorating the baptism of the Prince of Wales in 1842 is said to have been presented to members of the royal family by Queen Victoria.

In 1958, Queen Elizabeth's coronation was commemorated by a thimble bearing the letters E. R. (Elizabeth Regina) and the coronation crown.

An American commemorative thimble depicts the driving of the "Golden Spike" with a panoramic view of wagon trains to the iron horse.

A thimble commemorates the "World Columbian Exposition 1492-1892" at Chicago. The exposition was actually held in 1893 because buildings had not been completed in time for the four hundredth anniversary of the discovery of America.

Copper: Highly polished copper thimbles are popular among Scandinavian women.

Dates: A date is an interesting indication on a thimble whether this be a patent date or of some personal significance.

Floral: Many borders and designs are taken from nature and can be identified in groups.

Foreign: Thimbles from some foreign countries have particular characteristics. In a large collection, one may arrange groups according to country of origin.

Initials and names: Some unusual names popular in their time are preserved on thimbles. The type of engraving used is another facet of interest.

Jeweled: Jewels of many kinds have been used to decorate thimbles. Usually these are set in the rim where wear will not dislodge the stones.

Panoramic: Seascapes and landscapes were popular during the 19th century. These consistently present a peaceful setting. Boats, lighthouses, farms, and bridges were commonly used.

Plastic: Plain thimbles of plastic, manufactured in many colors with varying decorations, may be categorized in colorful displays.

Souvenir: Thimbles frequently bear enameled pictures as souvenirs. Subjects include the Vatican, Parthenon, Columbus Monument, a bridge in Sydney, Dutch windmills, and a Venetian gondola.

Thimble cases: Fine thimbles were frequently presented in a custom-made case. An ornamental holder of a thimble on the lady's dressing table afforded a feminine decor.

One thimble holder represents a small man wearing a purple hat (thimble) which tops a needle and thread container in the stand. This type of holder is similar to French novelties of the 19th century.

Chapter Ten

"JUST A THIMBLE FULL"

Small thimbles about two inches tall, made of fine old glass, silver, gold, and other metals, were popular novelties of the 19th century. These bear the inscriptions "Just a Thimble Full" or "Only a Thimble Full." Modern reproductions bear the same wording but experienced collectors recognize old glass by a smooth quality warm to the touch.

One of these gold cups bears Golden Wedding congratulations. Another is a souvenir of Victoria Falls, Africa.

In 1586, commemorative silver cups about five inches high were presented to members of the Tailors' Guild of Nuremberg, Germany. The cup is a copy of a thimble.

Japanese women wear a ring type metal thimble at the first joint.

Oriental thimbles are sometimes made of colored silk. These might seem clumsy to handle at first but they are sturdy.

It is said that ladies sometimes used their thimbles as a seal on letters in the days when most indentations on thimbles were handmade.

Initials are occasionally found in unique places. One gold thimble has what seems to be the insertion of a wedding band with the initials "EHP to MHP."

A silver thimble has "Priscilla" engraved in the apex.

In some European countries, thimbles are presented as confirmation gifts so that young ladies might start their hope chests.

Romantic intentions were deduced from the gift of a thimble. Its acceptance afforded encouragement to the suitor.

Finger shields of different metals were worn to protect the index finger of the hand opposite the one using the needle. Modern shields are reproduced in colored plastic.

Thimbles are sometimes used to commemorate anniversaries.

Interest in thimbles is not limited to women. Men take a scientific and historical interest in them. Men manufacture them.

On Thread-Needle Street in London is the Hall of Merchant Taylors' Company, incorporated in 1466. The peaceful settlement of a quarrel in 1485, commemorated annually, is a significant historical event.

Thimble-Knocking Street is said to have been the nickname of a street in an American city where ladies of the evening tapped thimbles against windows to attract passersby.

Thimbles sometimes bear religious references. One is inscribed I Tim. 6:12.

Among especially treasured thimbles is one issued to a Regular Army recruit, a volunteer, in 1917. The olive-drab colored sewing case contains needles, black and white thread, and an aluminum thimble. This was carried by Sergeant Ellis L. Isom during World War I.

A plain khaki colored plastic thimble purchased at an army surplus depot is said to have been used in World War II.

A small silver charm in the form of a thimble is frequently baked in a cake served at bridal showers.

In the Gay Nineties, gold thimbles set with diamonds were made to order by Simons Bros.

In 1897, the Sears Roebuck catalog advertised thimbles with some illustrations: "Aluminum thimbles 1 cent each; German silver thimbles 3 cents; solid silver 20 cents, with border 30 cents, engraved 45 cents, hand engraved 55 cents; gold filled 75 cents, engraved warranted $1.15; solid gold 10 K $1.90."

During the 18th and 19th centuries, flower and fruit designs implied prosperity.

Advertising Thimbles

Thimbles are a means of advertising that is a lasting reminder of the donor. Thimbles with names, addresses, and services are give-aways of interest to beginning collectors.

Plastics

Plastic thimbles advertise a wide variety of products and sometimes seek to focus attention on a candidate for political office. One thimble urges a vote for Richard Nixon as Senator. Sinclair Oil Company uses the dinosaur to advertise gasoline.

Miscellaneous

Among thimbles which seem unique and belong in no homogeneous group are the following:

A large white wooden thimble used by professional magicians to do tricks.

A souvenir thimble from California made of orangewood.

A hand forged iron thimble with crude wrinkled joining.

A sterling silver thimble with small ring at the top for fastening on a chatelaine.

A thimble patented in 1905 with movable needle threader and razor at the side to cut thread.

A thimble with small magnet to attract steel needle.

A novel thimble made in separate parts which fit into one another like an old fashioned collapsible drinking cup.

A thimble made of reindeer horn by an Eskimo in Alaska.

There must be something basic in the drive to collect things. This mysterious urge is similar to the impulse that kept Tycho Brahe, Dutch astronomer, charting the stars every night for 30 years in the 1500's. He derived enjoyment from his quest. He was fascinated with the recording of his nightly observations which resulted, years after his death, in the formulation of Kepler's laws.

In much the same way, collectors derive enjoyment from their quest for data and satisfaction from effort, whether or not the achievement is important.

$3,750 Thimble

Lillian Weiss' column The Antique Box in McCall's Magazine, December 1969, mentions that "Recently Christie Galleries in London sold at auction a one-half-inch-tall Meissen thimble made by the Famous Herold workshop during the early eighteenth century. Painted around its tiny circumference in the most precise detail is a miniature harbor scene showing six ships, thirty busy figures, six bales of cotton, and one large barrel. Price $3,750.

From consideration of extremes in craftsmanship and conditions, a myriad of avenues excite interest. The poorest and the richest invite respect. Therein lies the intrinsic value of inquiry which real collectors understand.

Thimbles are objects of affection. In themselves, they are not so important as the enrichment they afford.

Chapter Eleven

HINTS TO BEGINNING COLLECTORS

There can hardly be a better way to stimulate interest and encourage inquiry than by starting a collection. It can begin with one piece.

Thimbles in good condition are preferred but collectors sometimes buy old worn thimbles for certain features.

Duplicates are a good addition and may be used to trade with another collector.

Keep a catalog, a simple notebook, indicating the date acquired, name of donor or source, and description of thimble.

Display your collection and share your knowledge with others.

Attend antique and hobby shows.

Search the archives, libraries, and museums.

Study your pieces.

Communicate with other collectors.

Plastic thimbles are attractive and it is fun for the beginning collector to start categories of states, cities, colors, and subjects. Campaign data have long been collector's items and campaign thimbles seem to have been overlooked.

Thimble collecting frequently requires the aid of expert knowledge because so many fields are represented in this one small object.

Above all, enjoy the history, craftsmanship, sentiment, and romance to be found in thimbles.

Porcelain thimble holder, Dresden, Germany; 18th-19th century

The porcelain thimble, marked Royal Worcester, England, decorated with bluebirds and flowers, was a wedding gift.

Thimbles with Enamel

Top row:

(1) Denmark. Band of blue enamel showing farm scene with windmill. Modern. (2) Sterling, Simons Bros. Two narrow bands of white enamel, wide band of light blue enamel over a guilloche. (3) Sterling, Denmark. Band of blue enamel showing farm scene with windmill in panoramic effect.

Second row:

(1) Continental silver and enamel with amethyst top. Scene of Columbus monument in Barcelona, Spain. (2) Continental silver and enamel with simulated red stone top. Scene of St. Peter's Square, Rome. (3) Continental silver with enamel, simulated Mediterranean blue top. Scene of the Parthenon, Athens.

Third row:

(1) Continental silver. Enamel shield with arms. Puerto Rico. (2) Continental silver. Pale yellow enamel over a guilloche, carnelian top. (3) Continental silver. Enamel shield with boat scene and arms. Titisee, Germany.

Fourth row:

(1) Continental silver with enamel. Gondola scene, inscribed "Venezia". (2) Sterling. Band of white enamel over a guilloche with green ivy vine. (3) Sterling. Scenic band of enamel showing bridge in Sydney, Australia.

Fifth row:

(1) Collapsible sterling thimble with band of enamel over a guilloche. (2) Sterling with enamel sides, simulated green stone top. (3) Sterling, Simons Bros. Enamel band with dainty pink roses.

Thimbles of Silver

Top row: (1) Silver with wire work applied circles, chain and ring for finger. Unmarked, Turkey. Thimble resembles fez. (2) Mexican silver. Floral decoration on sides.

Second row: (1) Sterling, Simons Bros. Applied cherubs and garland. American. (2) Continental silver. Tall thimble, plain sides with fluted bands, waffle indentations on top. Engraved "E" in shaded hairline. (3) Panoramic scene of camel caravan at date palm oasis with pyramids in background. Unmarked.

Third row: (1) Heavy silver niello. Painted sailboat, buildings and monument. Hand pitted identations in top. Believed to be Russian. (2) Sterling, America. Birds and vine band. (3) Sterling, England. All-over floral top. (4) Sterling, commemorative, England. Coronation crown with "E" and "R", issued at coronation of Queen Elizabeth. (5) England. Commemorative thimble issued by Queen Victoria. Inscribed: "Prince of Wales Our Future Hope Heir to the British Throne, Born Nov. 9, 1841, Christened at Windsor Jan. 25, 1842".

Fourth row: (1) American, Simons Bros. Filigree, monogrammed "G. T. L.". (2) American, Simons Bros. Panoramic scene showing buffalo, Indians, trail-blazers, covered wagons, and the iron horse. Commemorates "The Golden Spike". (3) Wirework design filled with blue, white, and red enamel; 25 turquoise settings border the band at top and bottom. Believed to be Russian. (4) American, rococo, 1890's. Matching case. (5) American, Simons Bros. Cherubs and garland. Size 12.

Fifth row: (1) American, unmarked, commemorative. Inscribed: "World's Columbian Exposition 1492-1892". (2) Russian, prior to 1800. Inscribed with letter no longer used, niello or similar craftsmanship. (3) Mexican. Large with applied wirework. (4) Unmarked, all-over pansy design. (5) Exquisite ornate floral design applied to contrast background. Unmarked.

Sixth row: (1) Unmarked. Castle with stone wall and watch tower. Large bent pine tree may be symbolic. (2) Applied fleur-de-lis band with scalloped rim. May be French. (3) Italian wirework design on tall thimble. Small crystal perfume bottle fits into bottom of thimble. (4) Applied fleur-de-lis band applied to rim, leaving open scallops. Unmarked. May be French. (5) Sterling. Old dome-top thimble covered with settings of marquisette, gold lined.

Thimbles with Jewels

Precious and semi-precious stones have long been used to enhance the beauty of thimbles.

Top row: Continental silver, Italy. Ornate gilded band with polished coral settings. Late 19th century.

Second row: (1) Small continental silver, Italy. Gilded band with turquoise settings, lined with gold. (2) Bright-cut band simulating settings. (3) Continental silver, Italy. Turquoise settings, lined with gold.

Third row: (1) Continental silver, Italy. Turquoise settings, lined with gold. (2) Continental silver, Italy. Coral settings. (3) Brass, American. Applied butterfly with rhinestones.

Fourth row: (1) Italian. Applied band set with turquoise, lined with gold. (2) Italian. Applied band with green settings, lined with gold. (3) Italian. Applied band with turquoise settings, carnelian stone in top.

Fifth row: (1) and (2) Mexican. Narrow band of abalone at rim.

Thimbles of Gold

A gold thimble was a status symbol at sewing bees, the social circles of previous years.

Top row: (1) Wide rococo border, heavy gold. (2) Wide crescent border with forget-me-nots, engraved "Martha". (3) Simons Bros. Blossom and vine border. (4) Leaf and berry border, unmarked. (5) Simons Bros. Greek classic, fine beading.

Second row: (1) Diamond and panel design, indented beading, faceted rim. (2) Scene with castle on island. Unmarked, believed German. (3) Heavy gold paneled border on silver. (4) Classic band and rim, engraved "Addie". Unmarked. (5) Gunner Mfg. Gold band on silver, engraved "J.C.".

Third row: (1) Modern, unmarked. Chased hairline scroll on fluted contrast. (2) Simons Bros. Maple leaf. (3) Simons Bros. Gold band on sterling. (4) Handmade, triangle with eyelet, engraved "Leah Keller" in long name plate. (5) Solid gold, engraved "E H P to M H P". Unmarked.

Fourth row: (1) Simons Bros. Greek classic band engraved "Bertha". (2) Modified Empire design, scroll and floral, engraved "A. F." upside down. (3) Simons Bros. Foliage on contrast. (4) Brogan Silversmiths. Exquisitely engraved harbor scene. (5) G.S.C. Horseshoe and clover design.

Fifth row: (1) Unmarked. Exquisitely engraved buildings in medallions. (2) Simons Bros. Heavy band, modified Empire design, engraved "M" upside down. (3) Simons Bros. Applied gold paneled band, engraved "E. M." (4) Paneled geometric. (5) Lilies-of-the-valley and bowknot. Unmarked.

Thimbles with Stone Tops

Thimbles with amethyst, carnelian, goldstone, moonstone and other semi-precious stone tops may date to the 17th-18th century. Simulated stones are sometimes used in modern thimbles.

Top row: (1) Sterling, floral design, simulated stone, modern. (2) Sterling, simulated moonstone, Norwegian. Inscribed: "Greetings from Stavanger 1954".

Second row: (1) England. 18th-19th century. Goldstone top. (2) Continental silver, oval initial shield, deep engraving, amethyst top. (3) Continental silver with enamel, simulated stone top. Marked "Roma". Scene of St. Peter's Square.

Third row: (1) Continental silver, Sweden. Green top may be replacement. Inscribed "G.L.H." (2) Sterling, England. 18th-19th century. Engraved band with faceted rim, carnelian top. (3) Brass, fret band, amethyst top. (4) Silver with swag and oval design, carnelian top. 18th-19th century.

Fourth row: (1) German. Silver with gold band, exquisite engraving, pale amethyst top. Confirmation gift in Heidelberg. (2) Scandinavian, modern. Simulated red stone. (3) Continental silver with enamel, simulated Mediterranean blue top. Inscribed "Athens" in Greek. Scene of the Parthenon on reverse side.

Fifth row: (1) Continental silver. Design on band similar to old German thimbles, engraved "L.B.", shaded carnelian or amber top. (2) Continental silver with enamel. Inscribed: "Barcelona". Scene showing Columbus monument. Amethyst top. (3) Scandinavian silver. Embossed rose border, simulated blue stone, modern. (4) Germany. Modern, Continental silver, simulated green stone.

Sixth row: (1) Continental silver with colorful rose patterned enamel, green stone. (2) Scandinavian silver, modern. Simulated topaz. (3) Sterling from Sydney, Australia. All over floral sides, dark green shaded jade top. (4) Scandinavian silver. Spiral medallions, simulated red stone top.

Thimbles of Porcelain, Onyx, Ivory

Elegant porcelain thimbles represent masterful artistry. Luxurious rather than practical, bone china and porcelain thimbles add colorful beauty to a collection.

Top row: (1) Yellow rose pattern. Unmarked. (2) Yellow rose identical to first thimble but quality of china is finer. Unmarked.

Second row: (1) Royal Worcester Fine Bone China. Painted robin, signed "D. Perry". (2) Two bluebirds and spray of blossoms, marked "Royal Worcester England". (3) Pink and red roses with blue forget-me-nots and yellow blossom. Unmarked and unsigned.

Third row: (1) Old dome type thimble of Meissen china, Germany. Blue band, crossed sword maker's mark. Inscribed: "Ich dachte an dich in Meissen". Indentations are hand-made. (2) Modern ceramic thimble with rose, gold rim and top. Name "Myrtle" in gold.

Fourth row: (1) Bone china, made in England. Colorful fruit pattern with peach, grapes, plums. Signed J. Nussell. (2) Pale pink china, with rose, yellow and blue spray with blue ribbon. Unmarked. (3) Roses with forget-me-nots. Unmarked.

Fifth row: (1) Ivory. Very old. Plain wide border. No legible markings. Late 18th century. Indentations hand-made. (2) Onyx, carved from single piece. Shaded yellow and beige strata. (3) Ivory. Very old. Crisscross border, indentations hand-made.

Thimbles from Asia

Chinese and Japanese utilitarian thimbles are made of silk, brass, plastic and many metals. Ring type thimbles are worn low on the finger. Many Oriental thimbles are expandable.

Top row: (1) Handstitched lavender front and olive green back silk linen over padded cardboard. (2) Expandable band of leather with green plastic backing. Silk cord ties back ends together for correct size. (3) Plain cerise and apple green silk at front, brocaded dark green and apple green silk in back.

Second row: (1) Cerise and navy silk linen. (2) Expandable leather with red plastic backing. (3) Ring thimble, nickel, not expandable. (4) Leather with pink plastic backing. (5) Cerise, yellow, and navy blue plain silk linen, fourth part yellow brocade.

Third row: (1) All leather, expandable. (2) Pink plastic, expandable. (3) Blue plastic, expandable. (4) Red plastic, expandable. (5) Brass, expandable.

Fourth row: (1) Rose and green silk. (2) Lavender and navy blue silk. (3) Rose and lavender silk linen.

Fifth row: (1) Pink silk linen. Seam embroidered with bright green floss. (2) Green and rose silk linen. (3) White silk linen with woven pattern, stitched with pink floss.

Thimbles of Plastic

The appeal of color in advertising extends to plastic thimbles which are made in most colors of the spectrum.

Top row: (1) Plain blue. (2) White with red and blue printing. "Panama-Beaver Inked Ribbons." (3) Tan. "S. Harry Serwatt Associates, Realtors." (4) White campaign thimble. "Safeguard the Amercian Home, Nixon for U. S. Senator." (5) Pink. (6) Eggshell. "Helen Gates Bread." (7) Blue. "Thos. Jackson & Sons, Builders Supplies."

Second row: (1) Apple green, waffle indentations. (2) Russet, commemorative. "Eureka. 50th Anniversary." (3) Orange yellow. "The Celanese Tab is your Assurance of Quality." (4) White. "Panama-Beaver Inked Ribbons." (5) White with red top. "Monarch Ranges." (6) Pink. (7) Pale yellow.

Third row: (1) White. "Walker's Feeds." (2) Rose. (3) White. "Butter-Nut, the Coffee Delicious." (4) Yellow. "Beam World's Finest Bourbon." (5) Pale pink. (6) Tan. "Rainbow Laundry Inc." (7) Lavender.

Fourth row: (1) Tan. "Crown's." (2) Tall yellow. (3) White with red top. "Red E Popt Pop Corn." (4) White campaign. "Russell W. Root Your Next Mayor." (5) Tan. "Sinclair Oils" with dinosaur. (6) Cerise transparent. "Panama-Beaver Unimasters." (7) Green.

Fifth row: (1) Pink. "Beam World's Finest Bourbon since 1795." (2) White. "Mary Ann Silks and Woolens." (3) White. "The Plastic Center." (4) Tan. "Poll-Parrot Max Branovan Quality Shoes for Children." (5) White. (6) Transparent red. (7) White. "The Perma-Stone Corp."

Sixth row: (1) Dark red. (2) Pale pink. "The Plastic Center." (3) Blue. (4) Tan. "Filter Queen America's Bagless Cleaner." (5) Kelly green. (6) White with red print. "Stage Employes & Movie Operators." (7) White. "Sinclair Oils" with dinosaur.

Seventh row: (1) Blue, wide band. (2) Deep yellow. (3) White. "The 1-stop Sewing Shop Joe Gardner." (4) Yellow. (5) Beige. "Schumann & Co. Dry Cleaners." (6) White. "Badger Breeders Cooperative Breeding Better Cattle." (7) Red transparent.

Thimble Cases

A beautiful thimble was sometimes presented in an interesting custom made case.

Top row: (1) Carved bone case with matching thimble. (2) Celluloid sewing case with needles, thread and thimble. (3) Pincushion with thimble holder. (4) Celluloid thimble holder with needles and thread in stand. (5) Wood sewing case.

Second row: (1) Sterling acorn case. Unmarked. (2) Modern brass sewing kit with thimble. (3) Sterling thimble case. Marked Webster Co. (Now Reed & Barton).

Third row: (1) Hand stitched silk thimble case. Oriental. (2) Papier mache case with gilded top. (3) Basket with cover. (4) Leather case with thimble. Cape-town, Africa.

Fourth row: (1) Brass with gilt egg shaped case with red quilted lining. (2) Modern gold tone bird thimble holder. (3) Bone China thimble case. (4) Sterling pierced silver case, monogrammed T.J.R.

Fifth row: (1) Black wood thimble stand. The tall thimble is Italian wire work. The small crystal scent bottle fits into the base. (2) Slipper thimble holder, lined in purple velvet. (3) Slipper thimble holder with settings, lined in red velvet. (4) Blackthorn thimble case from Ireland. Harp and shamrocks carved on top and sides.

Sixth row: (1) Yellow enamel over a guilloche, carnelian in top of thimble. (2) Brass mesh case, decorated ends, jewels in clasp. Modern. (3) Leather case lined in dark blue velvet and pale blue silk, gilded fastener and hinges. (4) Sterling thimble case. England.

Thimbles with Names Engraved

A fine thimble with a name engraved is a precious, sentimental heirloom.

Top row:
(1) Sterling. Inscribed: "Tedie, Jonathan, Terry, Tom". (2) Sterling. Simons. Inscribed "Julia". (3) Sterling, English. Open-top, 15 butter-flies poised and in flight, inscribed "Mother". (4) Sterling, Ketcham-Mc-Dougall. Raised scroll border, inscribed "Helene". (5) Sterling, Ketcham McDougall. Currant design, inscribed "Pearl".

Second row:
(1) Sterling, scene of St. Peter's Square, Rome. Inscribed "Camelia". (2) Sterling. Inscribed "Annie". (3) Sterling. All-over floral design, inscribed "Doris". (4) Sterling. Plain, inscribed "Zylphia". (5) Sterling. Inscribed "Daisey".

Third row:
(1) Sterling. Plain with rolled rim. Inscribed "Jennie". (2) Sterling. Bamboo design on rim, inscribed "Abbie". (3) Sterling. Leaf and berry border, inscribed "May". (4) Sterling. Fan design, inscribed "Mina" upside down. (5) Sterling. Worn and bent, inscribed "Thuli".

Fourth row:
(1) Sterling. Open-top, wide scroll border, inscribed "Budie" or "Birdie". (2) Sterling, English. Geometric design on rim, inscribed "Lizzie". (3) Sterling. Grape design, inscribed "Hazel". (4) Sterling. Paneled border with leaf motif, inscribed "Katie". (5) Sterling. Aster border, inscribed "H. Lea".

Fifth row:
(1) Sterling. Fan border, inscribed "Alice". (2) Sterling. Maple leaf design, inscribed "Mabel 1893". (3) Sterling. Wide floral vine border, inscribed "Zana 1894".

Thimbles with Initials and Dates

Monograms or initials existed on signet rings thousands of years ago and dates are interesting clues.

Top row: (1) Sterling. Old English letters "E S T". (2) Sterling Gunner Mfg. "E M" in short hairline strokes, late 19th century. (3) Sterling, Simons Bros. "L M" in script. (4) Sterling, Simons Bros. Farm scene, "G. B." in shaded script. (5) Sterling, Brogan. Large ribbon letter "B".

Second row: (1) Sterling. Paneled with "L H" in hairline script. (2) Sterling, Webster Co. Shaded "A" in slanted script. (3) Sterling, Simons Bros. English text letters "H G" with crosslines. (4) Sterling. Monogram "MFR" in hairline letters. (5) Sterling, unmarked. Four borders, initials "E. S."

Third row: (1) Sterling. Unmarked, believed foreign, "E W". (2) Sterling. Initials "L P" in hairline script. (3) Sterling. "E P S" in cross line letters barely legible. (4) Sterling, Simons Bros. "A K" upside down in zigzag lines. (5) Sterling, England. Ring to fasten to chatelaine, small "G. R." in shaded script.

Fourth row: (1) Large silver thimble, believed to have come from India, letters "S B" and roman numerals at top. (2) Sterling. "Pearl" in shaded script. (3) "P. H." in script. (4) Inscribed "July 23, 1901". (5) Sterling. Inscribed "C & F".

Fifth row: (1) Novelty thimble with thread cutter at top, marked "Duke-Patented May 15, 1900". (2) Sterling. All-over floral pattern, inscribed "M to J" on rim. (3) Sterling. Cherubs and garlands, marked "Pat. Nov. 21, 1905". (4) Sterling. Souvenir thimble, "1492" Worlds Columbian Exposition 1892", size 11. (5) Sterling. Souvenir thimble, similar to next above but size 9. (The Chicago World Columbian Exposition was to have been held in 1892, the 400th anniversary of Columbus' discovery of America, but the buildings were not completed. The exposition was actually held in 1893.)

Thimbles with Scenes

Lighthouses, boats, and stone bridges were popular along the seacoast in Colonial times. Farm scenes linked by fences depicted a warm neighborliness. Scenic souvenir thimbles with names and dates are collectors' items.

Top row: (1) Brass, foreign. Wide border with applied castle and drawbridge. (2) Sterling, foreign. Bridge with towers, inscribed "E.H.". (3) Sterling, Gunner Mfg. Lighthouse and sailboat. (4) Sterling. Lighthouse and harbor, inscribed "F. P.". (5) Sterling, Simons Bros. Panoramic scene pictures sun in west, buffalo herd, Indian riders, campfire, covered wagon, and the iron horse, symbolizing the golden spike.

Second row: (1) Sterling, Simons Bros. Stone bridge, farm houses, mountains. (2) Sterling, Simons Bros. Millhouse, bridge, houses. (3) Sterling, Gunner Mfg. Bridge, boat. (4) Sterling. Harbor scene. (5) Sterling, Gunner Mfg. Church, pine trees, birds.

Third row: (1) Sterling. Lighthouse, sailboat, harbor. (2) Sterling, Simons Bros. Sunrise farm scene, fences, inscribed "L. M.". (3) Sterling, Simons Bros. Farmhouse, trees. (4) Sterling. Farm houses, mountains. (5) Sterling. Farmhouses, silos, mountains.

Fourth row: (1) Sterling. Castle with wrought-iron gates, dated Sept. 20, '81. (2) Sterling. Castle with gates and towers, initialed "F.C.C.". (3) Sterling. Harbor scene, beaded rim. (4) Sterling, Simons Bros. Farm houses, bridge, mill. (5) Sterling, Simons Bros. Farm houses, trees.

Fifth row: (1) Sterling. Panoramic scene on narrow rim, palm trees, houses. (2) Sterling, Simons Bros. Farm scene, sunset. (3) Sterling, Brogan. Harbor scene, rocky coast. (4) Sterling, Brogan. Harbor scene, building. (5) Sterling, English. Farm scene, mountains.

Thimbles with Borders

Top row: (1) Sterling. Wide zigzag border. (2) Sterling, Simons Bros. Zigzag pattern with floral design. (3) Sterling, Simons Bros. Wide ornate gothic border. (4) Sterling. Circle and crescent band. (5) Sterling. Paneled border, alternate rectangles with Indian designs.

Second row: (1) Sterling. Triangular design. (2) Sterling. Circle and crescent border. (3) Sterling. Rectangular panels, alternate diamond designs. (4) Continental silver. Line and fret, gold lined. (5) Sterling. Paneled border with circle and crescent.

Third row: (1) Sterling. Wide paneled border, shield and crescent. (2) Sterling. Rectangular panels with acanthus. (3) Sterling. Open-top, wide paneled decorated border. (4) Sterling. Paneled simple floral border. (5) Sterling. Wide paneled shell design.

Fourth row: (1) Sterling. Paneled dot and line design. (2) Sterling. Paneled floral. (3) Sterling. Narrow shell border, inscribed "Etta Age 20". (4) Sterling, Simons Bros. Paneled border, alternate brick tower design. (5) Sterling, Gunner Mfg. Border with faint zigzag pattern, beaded.

Fifth row: (1) Sterling. Wide floral scroll. (2) Sterling, Gunner Mfg. Ornate border of linked anchors, scroll band. (3) Sterling. Indian design, line and cross. (4) Sterling, Simons Bros. Circle and crescent border. (5) Brass. Circle and dot.

Thimbles with Floral Designs

Top row: (1) Sterling. Wide conventional vine border and rim, initials "P.Z.". (2) Sterling. Wide meshed floral border with beaded rim. (3) Sterling, Gunner Mfg. All-over floral cap, plain wide border. (4) Sterling, unmarked. Daisy border, small shield. (5) Sterling, Simons Bros. Conventional acanthus vine, beaded border.

Second row: (1) Sterling, Simons Bros. Birds and forget-me-nots. (2) Sterling. Wide chrysanthemum border, plain rim. (3) Sterling. Daisy border, domed top. (4) Sterling, Ketcham and McDougall. Meshed floral border, shield. (5) Sterling, Simons Bros. Birds and forget-me-nots.

Third row: (1) Continental silver, gold lined. Cosmos and leaf applied band, 18th century. (2) Sterling, Gunner Mfg. Applied dogwood band, shield. (3) Simons Bros. Forget-me-nots in medallions. (4) Sterling. S.B.C., grape and vine. (5) Sterling, Ketcham and McDougall. All-over floral cap, beaded rim.

Fourth row: (1) Sterling, Ketcham and McDougall. Wild rose, scroll shield. (2) Sterling. Applied narrow band with conventional flowers and leaf. (3) Sterling, Webster Co. Overlapping daisy design, applied rim. (4) Sterling, unmarked. Elegant border with convex medallions and flowers. (5) Sterling, Simons Bros. Medallions with flowers on contrast background.

Fifth row: (1) Sterling, England. All-over cap, 18th century. (2) Sterling. All-over floral, touchmarked (unknown). (3) Sterling. All-over floral scroll, unmarked, 18th century. (4) Sterling, Webster Co. 19th century, blossom and leaf. (5) Sterling. Triangular border with circle and dot, unmarked.

Thimbles with Floral Borders

During the 18th and 19th centuries, flower and fruit designs were symbols of prosperity, especially in European countries.

Top row: (1) Continental silver. Rosette. (2) Sterling. Lilies-of-the-valley. (3) Sterling. Clover and scroll, size 7. (4) Sterling, Simons Bros. Cosmos and vine, late 19th century. (5) Sterling, Simons Bros. Daisy, late 19th century.

Second row: (1) Sterling, Steel-Brussel Co., late 19th century. (2) Sterling, Simons Bros. Grape and leaf, 19th century. (3) Sterling. Daisy, unmarked. (4) Sterling, Webster Co. Overlapping daisies. (5) Sterling. Clover and festoons.

Third row: (1) Sterling. Cherry and leaf on contrast, unmarked. (2) Sterling, Simons Bros. Paneled leaf, late 19th century. (3) Sterling, Ketcham and McDougall. Currant design, late 19th century. (4) Sterling. S.B.C. leaf. (5) Sterling. Blossom border, circle and crescent band. 18th century.

Fourth row: (1) Sterling. S.B.C. leaf. (2) Sterling, Simons Bros. Hexagonal motif. (3) Sterling. Scroll and clover on contrast. (4) Sterling, Simons Bros. Wide geometric band, 19th century. (5) Sterling. Geometric medallions, unmarked.

Fifth row: (1) Sterling, Simons Bros. Patented May 31, 1898, elegant beaded border, inscribed "Priscilla" in apex. (2) Sterling. Sunflower and leaf on contrast, 19th century. (3) Sterling. Chrysanthemums on fluted border. (4) Sterling. UR, paneled, alternate cosmos. (5) Sterling. S.B.C. leaf, before 1904.

Thimbles with Geographical Identifications

Top row: (1) Brass, Germany. (2) Nickel. Engraved "Kamiah, Ida." (3) Stratnoid, England. (4) Brass, Germany. (5) Brass, England. Inscribed, " 'Her Majesty' Thimble". (6) Germany. Black stone at top. (7) Brass, Germany.

Second row: (1) Brass, Germany. Long. (2) Brass, England. " 'Her Majesty' Thimble". (3) Brass, Germany. (4) Nickel, England. (5) Nickel, England. (6) Blue enamel on sterling, lined with gold, Denmark. (7) Aluminum, Germany.

Third row: (1) Brass, Austria. (2) Brass, Australia. (3) Brass, England. (4) Gilded metal, all over lover's knot design, unmarked, Australia. (5) Brass, Austria. (6) Nickel, England. (7) Sterling, Germany.

Fourth row: (1) England. (2) Brass, Austria. (3) Brass, Germany. (4) Sterling, all-over floral, England. (5) Sterling, England. (6) Silver, Mexico. (7) White metal, currant vine, England.

Fifth row: (1) Sweden. "Stockholm". (2) Celluloid, England. Five painted cupids and garland. (3) Austria, silver. (4) Germany, silver. "Heidelberg". (5) Austria, brass. (6) Germany, sterling. Heavy applied band. (7) Stratnoid, England. Blue.

Sixth row: (1) Austria, brass. (2) Germany, brass. (3) Germany, brass. Painted border. (4) England, brass. (5) Germany, brass. Long. (6) Germany, brass. (7) Germany, brass.

Seventh row: (1) Wood, Africa. Believed to be mahogany. (2-7) Mexico. All silver, wire work, ornate sides.

Eighth row: (1) England, brass. Slanted fluting. (2) England, nickel. Diamond design. (3) Brass, Austria. (4) Enamel on wire, unmarked. (5) Sterling, England. (6) Silver, Mexico. (7) Silver, Mexico. Indian design, rope rim.

Thimbles with Various Rims and Borders

The diversity of designs in rims and borders enhances the collector's search.

Top row: (1) Simons Bros. Fan border. (2) Sterling. Plain rolled rim. (3) S.B.C. Circle and dot rim. (4) Sterling. Narrow fluted border, modern. (5) Narrow fluted border below line. (6) Sterling, England. Ring at top for chatelaine, worn faceted rim, 19th century.

Second row: (1) Plain border above fan and fluting, modern. (2) Plain border above fluting, modern. (3) Plain border above fan design. (4) Sterling, Simons Bros. Gadroon border, 19th century. (5) Plain band, fluting. (6) Wide border above fluting.

Third row: (1) Plain band above fluting, size 7. (2) Blossom and vine, 19th century. (3) Band inserted between hairline relief. (4) Sterling. Fan and line. (5) Plain band and fans, worn. (6) Simons Bros. Applied scroll rim, modern.

Fourth row: (1) S.B.C. Floral rim with small chip settings. (2) Simons Bros. Wide scroll border with matching rim, 19th century. (3) Sterling, unmarked. (4) Simons Bros. Fan. (5) Simons Bros. Scroll edge. (6) Wide border, fan, modern.

Fifth row: (1) Simons Bros. Scroll rim. (2) Ketcham and McDougall. Scroll rim, size 12 (similar to (1) but different silversmith), 19th century. (3) Simons Bros. elegant scroll on fluting. (4) Old dome topped thimble, unmarked. (5) Sterling. Plain band and fluting, unmarked. (6) Sterling. Slanted scroll with circles, unmarked.

Sixth row: (1) Narrow fan border, dotted line on rim, unmarked. (2) Unmarked, slightly peaked top, narrow fan. (3) Wide band inscribed "Delphi, Ind." and with "Lottie Griggs" engraved in hairline. (4) Sterling. Modern, plain with fluting. (5) Sterling. Squared geometric border. (6) Dot and leaf on fluting.

Seventh row: (1) Large, size 11, rounded top. (2) Slightly pointed top, beading below band. (3) Unusual, similar to overlay lettering "Delphi, Ind.". (4) Plain, sharp lines suggesting a top hat. (5) Size 12, narrow geometric border. (6) Leaf and berry border.

Thimbles of Brass

The variety of styles in utilitarian thimbles is a source of pleasure to the collector. Brass thimbles seldom bear maker's marks.

Top row: (1) Wide plain band, three tiers. (2) Plain band with beaded edge. (3) "Good Luck" on band. (4) Wide plain band, two tiers. (5) Plain band, heavy rim. (6) Three rows fluting. (7) Narrow fluting.

Second row: (1) Braided or faceted rim. (2) Zigzag border. (3) Wide band, fluting. (4) Palm fan design. (5) Fluting. (6) Heavy brass, applied rim. (7) Small Greek fan border.

Third row: (1) Fluting at top and bottom of band. (2) Plain band. (3) Three tiers. (4) Gadroon rim. (5) Four rows fluting. (6) Fluting. (7) Two tiers.

Fourth row: (1) Wide band, three tiers. (2) Wide band, fluting. (3) Wide band, narrow unpolished band. (4) Two tiers, hexagonal indentations. (5) Inscribed "THE PRUDENTIAL LIFE INSURANCE". (6) Elegant polished band, scroll design. (7) Classic design, fluting above, gadroon rim.

Fifth row: (1) Plain band, fluting. (2) Wide band, slanted fluting. (3) Elegant polished band, classic design, "Austria". (4) Four rows fluting, size 7. (5) Two tiers. (6) Three tiers. (7) Tailor's, narrow feather border.

Sixth row: (1) Child's thimble. (2) Zigzag on line contrast. (3) Fluting. (4) Fluting. (5) Modern brass, Japan. (6) Hole at rim for bracelet. (7) Elegant polished classic border.

Seventh row: (1) Plain band, fluting. (2) Three tier, wider demarcation at top. (3) Plain band, two rows fluting. (4) Modern Japanese. (5) Heavy polished brass, wide rim. (6) Wide band, one row fluting. (7) Wide band, zigzag narrow border.

Eighth row: (1) Plain band, three tiers, some white in indentations, (polishes to bright gold). (2) Plain brass with graduated sizes in rows of indentations. (3) Narrow rolled border at each side of band. (4) Marked "Japan". (5) Heavy brass, polished band. (6) Short tip, wide plain border. (7) Wide band with narrow fan trim.

Thimbles With Names, Places, or Services

Top row: (1) Japan. (2) Cathedral Drive, Lakewood, N. J. (3) State senator campaign, Pa. (4) Barrington, Ill. (5) Dillner Storage Co., Pgh. Pa.) (6) First National Life Insurance Co., New Orleans, La.

Second row: (1) Life and Casualty Ins. Co. Nashville. (2) Monticello Butane Gas Co. (2) Missouri Insurance Co., St. Louis, Mo. (4) Mary Ann Silks and Woolens, Evanston, Ill. (5) Stanley Home Products, Inc., Westfield, Mass. (red top). (6) Missouri Ins. Co., St. Louis, Mo. (pink).

Third row: (1) Lubri-Gas, Chicago. (2) Connecticut. (3) Office Supply Co., Books. (4) Baltimore Ins. Co. Sixtieth Anniversary. (5) Crown's, Chicago. (6) Real Silk Hosiery, Indianapolis, Ind.

Fourth row: (1) Real Silk Hosiery, Indianapolis, Ind. (2) Stanley Home Products, Westfield, Mass. (orange top). (3) Real Silk. (4) Real Silk. (5) Indiana Roofing. (6) Westfield, Mass.

Fifth row: (1) Galveston, Texas. (2) American Home Ins. Co., Topeka, Kansas (blue). (3) American Cleaners, Winnetka, Ill. (yellow). (4) Harry H. Kayne, Jeweler, Milwaukee, Wis. (5) Liberty Natl. Life Ins. Co., Birmingham, Ala. (6) Boost Boozer, Build Ala. (Pd. Pol. Adv.)

Sixth row: (1) Cash and Carry Laundry, Wilmette, Ill. (2) Beacon Cleaners, San Pedro. (3) Goldfish. (Milwaukee). (4) Evanston, Ill. (5) Chicago. (6) Real Silk (Ind.)

Seventh row: (1) Anderson Furn. Co. Dallas. (2) Toledo (Spain), upside down. (3) John Hancock Ins. Co., Boston. (4) Laundry, Wilmette. (5) Adjustadores True-Form (Havana). (6) Sabanas "Leda" (Havana).

Eighth row: (1) McAleavey & Co., Pt. Wash. (Wis.). (2) Real Silk, Ind. (3) Toledo (Spain). (4) Real Silk. (5) Merchants Co-op Bank, Boston. (6) Laundry, Wilmette.

Thimbles for Children

Small thimbles have been made for centuries. Children learned the alphabet making samplers, embroidering a sample of each letter and numeral.

At top: Two sterling charms.

Top row: (1) Sterling. Inscribed "The cow jumped over the moon", with illustrations engraved. (2) Fine heavy sterling, size 3. (3) Aluminum, with painted band, Goosey nursery rhyme. (4) Sterling with scroll border. (5) Sterling with squared faceted border.

Second row: (1) Brass with narrow attached rim (2) Sterling, geometric border, gadroon rim. (3) Brass, three bands polished, satiny finish. (4) Small aluminum thimble, embossed "Austria". (5) Brass, plain, American.

Third row: (1) Sterling, fan border, size 2. (2) Aluminum, plain. (3) Brass, inscribed "For a good girl". (4) Silver, Mexican, applied wire rim. (5) Brass, "M" impressed.

Fourth row: (1) Brass, heavy applied rim. (2) Brass, narrow geometric border. (3) Brass. Found used as doorknob on old clock. (4) Sterling, indentations graduated. (5) Aluminum, plain.

Fifth row: (1) (2) and (3) pewter, (4) brass, (5) pewter, all inscribed "For a Good Girl".

Sixth row: (1) (2) and (3) brass, all inscribed "For a Good Girl". (4) Aluminum, plain. (5) Brass, fluted border.

Thimbles with Open Tops

Open top thimbles are called tailor's thimbles. These are usually worn on the thumb. Dressmakers may prefer an open top because the fingertip is free to feel the needle and material.

Top row: (1) Sterling, size 12. (2) Nickel with large indentations for heavy sewing. (3) Sterling, size 11, marked "A L & Co", oval shape. (4) Nickel, fluted border. (5) Old iron thimble.

Second row: (1) Steel. (2) Iron lined with aluminum. (2) Iron. (3) Iron with large numeral 2 on rim. Worn through at third row from top. (5) Steel with aluminum lining.

Third row: (1) Sterling with narrow fan border. (2) Iron lined with aluminum. (3) Iron, crude joining. (4) Nickel. (5) Nickel, fluted trim.

Fourth row: (1) White metal. (2) White metal. (3) Sterling, marked "10" on rim, large hexagonal indentations. (4) Sterling, 9, hexagonal indentations. (5) Sterling, scroll on fluted border, beaded rim.

Fifth row: (1) Heavy steel, large indentations, for thick fabrics. (2) Sterling, size 8, worn through at third row from top. (3) White metal, worn through third row from top. (4) Iron, hand forged. (5) Heavy steel.

Sixth row: (1) Nickel. (2) Heavy steel. (3) Nickel. (4) Iron. (5) Heavy iron crudely seamed.

Advertising with Aluminum Thimbles

Aluminum thimbles come in a wide variety of shapes, sizes, bands and colors, as well as print identifying places, donors and services.

Top row: (1) Modern, elongated indentations, blue band. (2) Modern three tiered, red band. (3) Noll Piano Co. (4) Mrs. Karl's Fine Bread. (5) Plain fluted border. (6) Unity Dye Works. (7) "Thank You" Palmetier & Abell.

Second row: (1) Blazer Oil Co. (2) Myers Furniture Co. (3) Hoover Home Happiness. (4) Eagle Laundry. (5) Red Diamond Coffee. (6) Modern Kitchens Inc. (7) Singer Sewing Machines.

Third row: (1) Modern Kitchens Inc. (Milwaukee). (2) Sands Gas Water Heaters. (3) Star Cleaners, Humboldt 9321. (4) Cadillac Electric Vacuum Cleaners. (5) Drive a Buick. (6) Star Brand Shoes. (7) Use I-H Flour.

Fourth row: (1) Wide band, fluted. (2) Mrs. Karl's Fine Bread. (3) Singer Sewing Machines. (4) Singer Sewing Machines. (5) Delco Light Lightens the Burden of the Housewife. (6) Star Brand Shoes. (7) Modern Kitchens Inc.

Fifth row: (1) International Harvester. (2) Yellow Cab. (3) Mid-City Trust and Savings Bank. (4) Round Oak Furnaces. (5) Pieper's Gargoyle Coffee. (6) Hirschman's Dairy. (7) For Goodness Sake—Wait For Watkins, Use Watkins Products.

Sixth row: (1) Purity Nut Margarin. (2) Maxwell House Coffee. (3) Soft Water Laundry. (4) Nu-Way Laundry and Cleaners. (5) Dearborn Laundry. (6) Holland Furnaces Make Warm Friends. (7) La Casa Americana (Havana).

Seventh row: (1) Be Sure With Pure. (2) The Emrick Co. Undertakers, Inc. (3) Bonanza Coffee, It's Great. (4) Pieper's Gargoyle Coffee. (5) Sheridan Laundry. (6) Old Reliable Coffee. (7) Wm. Klug & Sons (embossed Austria).

Eighth row: (1) Excelsior Laundry. (2) Sands Gas Water Heaters. (3) Faust Beauty Preparations. (4) Use I-H Flour. (5) Pieper's Gargoyle Coffee. (6) North American Union Life Assurance Society. (7) Drive a Buick.

Thimble Novelties

Top row: (1) Thimble with razor for cutting thread, and wire needle threader. Marked Pat. 9. American. (2) Thimble holder with needles and thread inside. (3) Finger shield patented April 10, 1860, and April 2, 1861. (4) Purple thimble holder with needles and thread inside. (5) Thimble with razor and wire needle threader.

Second row: (1) Modern black celluloid finger shield. Canadian. (2) Thimble with razor and needle threader. (3) Large white wood magician's thimble for tricks. (4) Brass thimble with thread cutter and small unidentified device. Patented April 14, 1885. (5) Blue celluloid finger shield. Canadian.

Third row: (1) Modern nickel thimble with double thread cutter. (2) Orangewood souvenir thimble marked "Los Angeles, Cal." (3) Wood. (4) Ivory. (5) Modern. Double thread cutter.

Fourth row: (1) Small modern thimble with single thread cutter. (2) Double cutter. (3) Carved bone thimble. (4) Thimble with disc in center of apex with slot around edge to protect long fingernails. (5) Modern single thread cutter.

Fifth row: (1) Thimble with single cutter. (2) Thimble with razor and needle threader. (3) Thimble with disc to protect long fingernails.

World War I Thimble

The olive-drab thimble kit issued to Regular Army recruit (a volunteer) Ellis L. Isom at Jefferson Barracks, St. Louis, Missouri, in 1917, bears patent dates May 25, 1909, and January 1912, manufactured by the In-Spool Mfg. Co. N. Y., USA.

The thimble served faithfully with its owner on Mexican Border duty; at Fort Bliss, El Paso, Texas; Camp MacArthur, Waco, Texas; Toronto and Montreal, Canada; Boston, Mass.; New York City and Camp Merritt, N. J.

Travels included the transport America (captured German liner, Amerika), Liverpool, London, Dover, and Brest. There were special missions to Spain, Italy, and Belgium; then Paris and Langres before front line action at Cantigney and Soissons. After rest at Fluvy (Haute Marne), more fireworks at St. Mihiel and the Meuse Argonne. The only address permitted was "A.E.F. France". The only two locations where they had a real roof over their heads were a barn loft in Fulvy and Fort Bonnelle at Langres. The pup-tents, dugouts, and woods, or brush shelters bore no formal addresses.

This soldier with thimble then found himself in hospitals at Langres, Chaumont, and Bordeaux. After a stormy trip on the hospital ship Pastores, he was stationed at hospitals at Camp Stuart, Newport News, Va., and Fort Sheridan, Ill.

Sgt. Ellis L. Isom (1025584) who served in the 34 Infantry, Seventh Division; 16th Infantry, First Division; 11th Company, 3rd Bn. A.C.S. was honorably discharged as "Sergeant of Infantry—Unassigned." He is a member of Society of The First Division; life member, Disabled American Veterans; American Legion; the Forty and Eight; Veterans of Foreign Wars; Military Order of The Cootie; and Veterans of World War I.

The thimble is aluminum with wide band of fluting. The kit contains needles, pins, white, black and olive-drab thread. One needle is still threaded.

Illustrations from Victoria and Albert Museum, London.

Left to right: Four English enamel thimbles. *First*, painted with sprays of flowers on
        colors. Gilt metal rim.
        Second, painted with sprays of flowers in colors in panels enclosed by
        raised white scrolls and reserved on an apple green ground. Gilt metal rim.
        Third, painted in colors and gilt with small landscape reserved on a tur-
        quoise blue ground. Gilt metal rim.
        Fourth, painted with sprays of flowers in colors and crimson scrolls. Gilt
        metal rim. All these enamels above were made in Bilston, Wednesbury
        Staffordshire during the second half of the 18th century.

Thimble at center: Silver: The body is of filigree openwork and scrolls. Believed to be
        Italian. 18th century.

Bottom row left to right: Needlecase, chased silver in the form of a pestle. Augsburg, Ger-
        many, 17th century.
        Italian filigree. 18th century.
        Box, thimble and needlecase. All silver-gilt, covered with openwork scrolls
        filled in with colored enamels. German, 18th century.
        Victoria and Albert Museum, London.

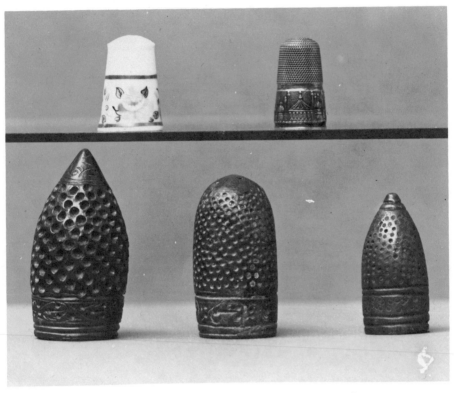

Illustrations from Victoria and Albert Museum, London.

Left to right: English porcelain thimble. 18th century.
English silver thimble, stamped with view of Royal Pavilion. Brighton.
19th century.

Left to right: Cast bronze thimble, from Cordoba, Hispano-Moresque. 12th/13th century.
Two cast bronze thimbles as above but from Granada.

91